The Song
that Sings
the Bird

for

Elsa Grant

in long and loving friendship

William Collins Sons & Co Ltd
London · Glasgow · Sydney · Auckland
Toronto · Johannesburg

First published 1989

© this collection Ruth Craft 1989
© illustrations John Vernon Lord 1989

A CIP catalogue record for this book is
available from the British Library.

ISBN 0 00 191283 6

Printed and bound in Great Britain by
Hartnolls, Bodmin, Cornwall

The Song
that Sings
the Bird

Poems for young children

chosen by Ruth Craft

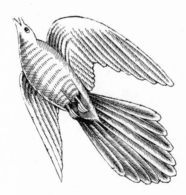

Illustrations by John Vernon Lord

Collins

When I was about eight, I was given a book called *Poems for Youth*. It was a dark dingy green. It had very small print and no pictures. I got a terrible telling off for trying to draw pictures all over the words with my crayons and for putting a big purple tick beside the poems I liked best.

I could read some of the poems for myself but others were too complicated and grown ups read them to me. I didn't like that creepy polite voice they used when they read them but I liked some of the poems. I loved the words. I loved the way they crashed together or came together gently to make a rhyme. I liked the way a poem was often jam-packed full of ideas, feelings, sights and sounds so that it made picture after picture in your mind.

One of the things I still like about poetry is the way the poet grabs all your attention in one go. Story-tellers spin things along to keep your attention and I like that too, but a poet has a way of making things sharp and concentrated and full of flavour. Perhaps that's why Vernon Scannell talks about writing his poem with a "marmite nibbed forefinger". I hope you'll find some poems with plenty of bite in this collection.

The other thing I hope you'll find is plenty of variety. You'll find poems about families, friends, frogs and foxgloves. You'll find a poem about that awful moment in the classroom when you can't find anything to write about and that good moment when you realise that having a brother or sister to share with is OK. You'll find poems where the poet is pulling your leg and you know he or she is pulling your leg so that's half the fun of it. And you'll find poems where the poet asks you to be quite still and concentrate hard on a hawthorn tree, the cold loneliness of fishing by yourself or the secret, silent growth of mushrooms in the dark.

I hope I've left you plenty of room to move around and find what you like in this book. One of the good things about a book of poetry is that you don't have to start at the beginning and go on until you come to the end. You can just dip in and out as you like.

I hope it will please you to dip into this collection over and over again.

Ruth Craft

· CONTENTS ·

· CONTENTS ·

· CONTENTS ·

I am the Song

I am the song that sings the bird.
I am the leaf that grows the land.
I am the tide that moves the moon.
I am the stream that halts the sand.
I am the cloud that drives the storm.
I am the earth that lights the sun.
I am the fire that strikes the stone.
I am the clay that shapes the hand.
I am the word that speaks the man.

CHARLES CAUSLEY

The Door

Go and open the door.
  Maybe outside there's
  a tree, or a wood,
  a garden,
  or a magic city.

Go and open the door.
  Maybe a dog's rummaging.
  Maybe you'll see a face,
or an eye,
or the picture
        of a picture.

Go and open the door.
  If there's a fog
  it will clear.

Go and open the door.
  Even if there's only
  the darkness ticking,
  even if there's only
  the hollow wind,
  even if
        nothing
        is there,
go and open the door.

At least
there'll be
a draught.

MIROSLAV HOLUB
translated by Ian Milner and George Theiner

I saw a Peacock with
a Fiery Tail

I saw a Peacock with a fiery tail,
I saw a blazing Comet drop down hail,
I saw a Cloud with ivy circled round,
I saw a sturdy Oak creep on the ground,
I saw a Pismire swallow up a whale,
I saw a raging Sea brim full of ale,
I saw a Venice Glass sixteen foot deep,
I saw a Well full of men's tears that weep,
I saw their Eyes all in a flame of fire,
I saw a House as big as the moon and higher,
I saw the Sun even in the midst of night,
I saw the Man that saw this wondrous sight.

ANON

from *The Dragon Speaks*

'Now I keep watch on the gold in my rock cave
In a country of stones: old, deplorable dragon,
Watching my hoard. In winter night the gold
Freezes through toughest scales my cold belly.
The jagged crowns and twisted cruel rings
Knobbly and icy are old dragon's bed.

Often I wish I hadn't eaten my wife,
Though worm grows not to dragon till he eat worm.
She could have helped me, watch and watch about,
Guarding the hoard. Gold would have been the safer.
I could uncoil my weariness at times and take
a little sleep, sometimes when she was watching.

Last night under the moonset a fox barked,
Woke me. Then I knew I had been sleeping.
Often an owl flying over the country of stones
Startles me, and I think I must have slept.
Only a moment. That very moment a man
Might have come out of the cities, stealing,
   to get my gold.'

C.S. LEWIS

Poem on Bread

The poet is about to write a poem:
He does not use a pencil or a pen.
He dips his long thin finger into jam
Or something savoury preferred by men.
This poet does not choose to write on paper,
He takes a single slice of well-baked bread
And with his jam or marmite-nibbed forefinger
He writes his verses down on that instead.
His poem is fairly short as all the best are.
When he has finished it he hopes that you
Or someone else – your brother, friend or sister –
Will read and find it marvellous and true.
If you can't read, then eat: it tastes quite good.
If you do neither, all that I can say
Is he who needs no poetry or bread
Is really in a devilish bad way.

VERNON SCANNELL

The Magic Box

I will put in the box

the swish of a silk sari on a summer night,
fire from the nostrils of a Chinese dragon,
the tip of a tongue touching a tooth.

I will put in the box

a snowman with a rumbling belly,
a sip of the bluest water from Lake Lucerne,
a leaping spark from an electric fish.

I will put in the box

three violet wishes spoken in Gujarati,
the last joke of an ancient uncle
and the first smile of a baby.

I will put in the box

a fifth season and a black sun,
a cowboy on a broomstick
and a witch on a white horse.

My box is fashioned from ice and gold and steel,
with stars on the lid and secrets in the corners.
Its hinges are the toe joints
of dinosaurs.

I shall surf in my box
on the great high-rolling breakers of the wild Atlantic,
then wash ashore on a yellow beach
the colour of the sun.

KIT WRIGHT

The Penny Fiddle

Yesterday I bought a penny fiddle
   And put it to my chin to play,
But I found that the strings were painted
   So I threw my fiddle away.

A little red man found my fiddle
   As it lay abandoned there;
He asked me if he might keep it,
   And I told him I did not care.

But he drew such music from the fiddle
   With help of a farthing bow
That I offered five guineas for the secret
   But, alas, he would never let it go.

ROBERT GRAVES

Gulliver in Lilliput

From his nose
Clouds he blows.
When he speaks,
Thunder breaks.
When he eats,
Famine threats.
When he treads,
Mountains' heads
Groan and shake;
Armies quake.
See him stride
Valleys wide,
Over woods,
Over floods.
Troops take heed,
Man and steed:
Left and right,
Speed your flight!
In amaze
Lost I gaze
Toward the skies:
See! and believe your eyes!

ALEXANDER POPE

The Paint Box

'Cobalt and umber and ultramarine,
Ivory black and emerald green—
What shall I paint to give pleasure to you?'
'Paint for me somebody utterly new.'

'I have painted you tigers in crimson and white,'
'The colours were good and you painted aright.'
'I have painted the cook and a camel in blue
And a panther in purple.' 'You painted them true.'

Now mix me a colour that nobody knows,
And paint me a country where nobody goes,
And put in it people a little like you,
Watching a unicorn drinking the dew.'

E.V. RIEU

The Key of the Kingdom

This is the Key of the Kingdom:
In that Kingdom there is a city;
In that city is a town;
In that town there is a street;
In that street there winds a lane;
In that lane there is a yard;
In that yard there is a house;
In that house there waits a room;
In that room an empty bed;
And on that bed a basket –
A basket of sweet flowers:
Of flowers, of flowers;
A basket of sweet flowers.

Flowers in a basket;
Basket on the bed;
Bed in the chamber;
Chamber in the house;
House in the weedy yard;
Yard in the winding lane;
Lane in the broad street;
Street in the high town;
Town in the city;
City in the Kingdom –
This is the Key of the Kingdom.
    Of the Kingdom this is the Key.

ANON

An Emerald is as Green as Grass

An emerald is as green as grass;
  A ruby red as blood;
A sapphire shines as blue as heaven;
  A flint lies in the mud.

A diamond is a brilliant stone,
  To catch the world's desire;
An opal holds a fiery spark;
  But a flint holds fire.

CHRISTINA ROSSETTI

The Sea

The sea is a hungry dog,
Giant and grey.
He rolls on the beach all day.
With his clashing teeth and shaggy jaws
Hour upon hour he gnaws
The rumbling, tumbling stones,
And 'Bones, bones, bones, bones!'
The giant sea-dog moans,
Licking his greasy paws.

And when the night wind roars
And the moon rocks in the stormy cloud,
He bounds to his feet and snuffs and sniffs,
Shaking his wet sides over the cliffs,
And howls and hollos long and loud.

But on quiet days in May or June,
When even the grasses on the dune
Play no more their reedy tune,
With his head between his paws
He lies on the sandy shores,
So quiet, so quiet, he scarcely snores.

JAMES REEVES

Early in the Morning

Early in the morning
The water hits the rocks,
The birds are making noises
Like old alarum clocks,
The soldier on the skyline
Fires a golden gun
And over the back of the chimney-stack
Explodes the silent sun.

CHARLES CAUSLEY

The Writer of this Poem

The writer of this poem
Is taller than a tree
As keen as the North wind
As handsome as can be

As bold as a boxing-glove
As sharp as a nib
As strong as scaffolding
As tricky as a fib

As smooth as a lolly-ice
As quick as a lick
As clean as a chemist-shop
As clever as a

The writer of this poem
Never ceases to amaze
He's one in a million billion
(Or so the poem says!)

ROGER McGOUGH

Pink Azalea

I feel as though
this bush were grown
especially for me.
I feel as though
I almost am
this little flowering tree.

CHARLOTTE ZOLOTOW

Foxgloves

Foxgloves on the moon keep to dark caves.
They come out at the dark of the moon only and in waves
Swarm through the moon-towns and wherever there's
  a chink
Slip into the houses and spill all the money, clink-clink,
And crumple the notes and re-arrange the silver dishes,
And dip hands into the goldfish bowls and stir the goldfishes,
And thumb the edges of the mirrors, and touch the sleepers
Then at once vanish into the far distance with a wild laugh
  leaving the house smelling faintly of Virginia Creepers.

TED HUGHES

Fishing Vessel

The hawthorn tree
   that trawled its catch

of crimson berries
   in its scratchy net

a wild way out
   in the rending winds

dreams at anchor
   but soon will hoist

its new white sails
   on the late spring tide.

KIT WRIGHT

Loveliest of Trees
(from *A Shropshire Lad*)

Loveliest of trees, the cherry now
Is hung with bloom along the bough,
And stands about the woodland ride
Wearing white for Eastertide.

Now, of my threescore years and ten,
Twenty will not come again,
And take from seventy springs a score,
It only leaves me fifty more.

And since to look at things in bloom
Fifty springs are little room,
About the woodlands I will go
To see the cherry hung with snow.

A.E. HOUSMAN

Mushrooms

Overnight, very
Whitely, discreetly,
Very quietly
Our toes, our noses
Take hold of the loam,
Acquire the air.

Nobody sees us,
Stops us, betrays us;
The small grains make room.

Soft fists insist on
Heaving the needles,
The leafy bedding.

Even the paving;
Our hammers, our rams,
Earless and eyeless.

Perfectly voiceless,
Widen the crannies,
Shoulder through holes. We
Diet on water,
On crumbs of shadow,
Bland-mannered, asking

Little or nothing.
So many of us!
So many of us!

We are shelves, we are
Tables, we are meek,
We are edible,

Nudgers and shovers
In spite of ourselves.
Our kind multiplies;

We shall by morning
Inherit the earth.
Our foot's in the door.

SYLVIA PLATH

First Day at School

A millionbillionwillion miles from home
Waiting for the bell to go. (To go where?)
Why are they all so big, other children?
So noisy? So much at home they
must have been born in uniform
Lived all their lives in playgrounds
Spent the years inventing games
that don't let me in. Games
that are rough, that swallow you up.

And the railings.
All around, the railings.
Are they to keep out wolves and monsters?
Things that carry off and eat children?
Things you don't take sweets from?
Perhaps they're to stop us getting out
Running away from the lessins. Lessin.
What does a lessin look like?
Sounds small and slimy.
They keep them in glassrooms.
Whole rooms made out of glass. Imagine.

I wish I could remember my name
Mummy said it would come in useful.
Like wellies. When there's puddles.
Yellowwellies. I wish she was here.
I think my name is sewn on somewhere
Perhaps the teacher will read it for me.
Tea-cher. The one who makes the tea.

ROGER McGOUGH

maggie and milly and
molly and may

maggie and milly and molly and may
went down to the beach (to play one day)

and maggie discovered a shell that sang
so sweetly she couldn't remember her troubles, and

milly befriended a stranded star
whose rays five languid fingers were;

and molly was chased by a horrible thing
which raced sideways while blowing bubbles: and

may came home with a smooth round stone
as small as a world and as large as alone.

For whatever we lose (like a you or a me)
it's always ourselves we find in the sea

E.E. CUMMINGS

Mean Song

Snickles and podes,
Ribble and grodes:
That's what I wish you.

A nox in the groot,
A root in the stoot
And a gock in the forbeshaw, too.

Keep out of sight
For fear that I might
Glom you a gravely snave.

Don't show your face
Around any place
Or you'll get one flack snack in the bave.

EVE MERRIAM

Marigold Pie

'Say what you will,
You won't pass by
If you can't make a
Marigold pie.'

'Let me pass!
I don't lie
And I can make a
Marigold pie.'

'Marigold petals.
Two small stones,
Lawn-grass clippings,
Chicken bones,
A spider's web with one dead fly
All mixed up in the wink of an eye.
And here it is for you to try.'

'Thanks, but no thanks – pass on by.'

DENNIS DOYLE

Write a Poem

'Write a poem' our teacher said
'A poem about an animal or a place,
Something that happened to you
In the holidays.
Better still write about yourself.
What you feel like,
What's inside you
And wants to come out'.
Stephen straightaway
Began to write slowly
And went on and on
Without looking up.
John sighed and looked far away
Then suddenly snatched up his pen
And was scribbling and scribbling.
Ann tossed back her long hair
And smiled as she began.
But I sat still.
I thought of fighting cats
With chewed ears
And dogs sniffing their way along
Windy streets strewn with paper
But there seemed nothing new
To say about them . . .
The holidays? Nothing much happened.
And what's inside me?
Only the numbness of cold fingers.
The grey of the sky today.
John sighed again.
Peter coughed.

Papers rustled.
Pens scratched.
A blowfly was fuzzing
At a window pane.
The tittering clock
Kept snatching the minutes away
I had nothing to say.

OLIVE DOVE

The Boy Fishing

I am cold and alone,
On my tree-root sitting as still as stone.
The fish come to my net. I scorned the sun,
The voices on the road, and they have gone.
My eyes are buried in the cold pond, under
The cold, spread leaves; my thoughts are silver-wet.
I have ten stickleback, a half-day's plunder,
Safe in my jar. I shall have ten more yet.

E.J. SCOVELL

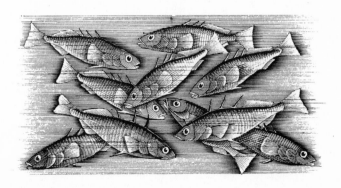

London City

I have London, London, London –
All the city, small and pretty,
In a dome that's on my desk, a little dome.
I have Nelson on his column
And Saint Martin-in-the-Fields
And I have the National Gallery
And two trees,
And that's what London is – the five of these.

I can make it snow in London
When I shake the sky of London;
I can hold the little city small and pretty in my hand;
Then the weather's fair in London,
In Trafalgar Square in London,
When I put my city down and let it stand.

RUSSELL HOBAN

Stupidity Street

I saw with open eyes
Singing birds sweet
Sold in the shops
For the people to eat,
Sold in the shops of
Stupidity Street.

I saw in vision
The worm in the wheat,
And in the shops nothing
For people to eat;
Nothing for sale in
Stupidity Street.

RALPH HODGSON

The Firemen

Clang! Clang! Clang!
Says the red fire bell –
'There's a big fire blazing
At the Grand Hotel!'

The firemen shout
As they tumble out of bed
And slide down the pole
To the fire engine shed.

The fire engine starts
With a cough and a roar
And they all climb aboard
As it shoots from the door.

The firemen's helmets,
The ladders and hoses,
Are brassy and bright
As a jug full of roses.

Whee! Whee! Whee! –
You can hear the cry
Of the siren shrieking
As they hurtle by.

At the Grand Hotel
There is smoke and steam.
Flames at the windows
And people who scream.

The biggest fireman
Carries down
A fat old lady
In her dressing gown.

When the fire is finished
The firemen go
Back through the same streets
Driving slow.

Home at the station
The firemen stay
And polish up the nozzles
For the next fire day.

JAMES K. BAXTER

Salford Road

Salford Road, Salford Road,
Is the place where I was born,
With a green front gate, a red brick wall
And hydrangeas round a lawn.

Salford Road, Salford Road,
Is the road where we would play
Where the sky lay over the roof tops
Like a friend who'd come to stay.

The Gardeners lived at fifty-five,
The Lunds with the willow tree,
Mr Pool with the flag and the garden pond
And the Harndens at fifty-three.

There was riding bikes and laughing
Till we couldn't laugh any more,
And bilberries picked on the hillside
And picnics on the shore.

I lay in bed when I was four
As the sunlight turned to grey
And heard the train through my pillow
And the seagulls far away.

And I rose to look out of my window
For I knew that someone was there
And a man stood as sad as nevermore
And didn't see me there.

And when I stand in Salford Road
And think of the boy who was me
I feel that from one of the windows
Someone is looking at me.

My friends walked out one Summer day,
Walked singing down the lane,
My friends walked into a wood called Time
And never came out again.

We live in a land called Gone-Today
That's made of bricks and straw
But Salford Road runs through my head
To a land called Evermore.

GARETH OWEN

Snow and Sun

White bird, featherless,
Flew from Paradise,
Pitched on the castle wall;

Along came Lord Landless;
Took it up handless,
And rode away horseless to the King's white hall.

ANON

Weather

Dot a dot dot dot a dot dot
Spotting the windowpane.

Spack a spack speck flick a flack fleck
Freckling the windowpane.

A spatter a scatter a wet cat a clatter
A splatter a rumble outside.

Umbrella umbrella umbrella umbrella
Bumbershoot barrell of rain.

Slosh a galosh slosh a galosh
Slither and slather a glide

A puddle a jump a puddle a jump
A puddle a jump puddle splosh

A juddle a pump a luddle a dump
A pudmuddle jump in and slide!

EVE MERRIAM

The Great Rain is Over
(from *Evening*)

The great rain is over,
  The little rain begun,
Falling from the higher leaves,
  Bright in the sun,
Down to the lower leaves,
  One drop by one.

MARY COLERIDGE

Cat and the Weather

Cat takes a look at the weather.
Snow.
Puts a paw on the sill.
His perch is piled, is a pillow.

Shape of his pad appears.
Will it dig? No.
Not like sand.
Like his fur almost.

But licked, not liked,
Too cold.
Insects are flying, fainting down.
He'll try

to bat one against the pane.
They have no body and no buzz.
And now his feet are wet:
it's a puzzle.

Shakes each leg,
then shakes his skin
to get the white flies off.
Looks for his tail,

tells it to come on in
by the radiator.
World's turned queer
somehow. All white,

no smell. Well, here
inside it's still familiar.
He'll go to sleep until
it puts itself right.

MAY SWENSON

Bite, frost, bite!
(from *Winter*)

Bite, frost, bite!
You roll up away from the light
The blue wood-louse, and the plump dormouse,
And the bees are stilled, and the flies are killed,
And you bite hard into the heart of the house,
But not into mine.

ALFRED, LORD TENNYSON

Wind

I pulled a hummingbird out of the sky one day
    but let it go,
I heard a song and carried it with me
    on my cotton streamers,
I dropped it on an ocean and lifted up a wave
    with my bare hands,
I made a whole canefield tremble and bend
    as I ran by,
I pushed a soft cloud from here to there,
I hurried a stream along a pebbled path,
I scooped up a yard of dirt and hurled it in the air,
I lifted a straw hat and sent it flying,
I broke a limb from a guava tree,
I became a breeze, bored and tired,
and hovered and hung and rustled and lay
    where I could.

DIONNE BRAND

Rapunzel

'Rapunzel, Rapunzel,
Let down your golden hair!
How can I climb to your window
Without a stair?'

'If you fall from my tower, prince,
You will break your bones.
There are thorn bushes all around it
And hard, rough stones.'

'Whether or not I fall
I do not care;
But let down the swinging ladder
Of your bright hair.'

'The witch who holds me captive
On an eagle's back she flies;
If she came now she would beat me
And put out your eyes.'

'There's nothing I like the look of
When you're not there.
Rapunzel, Rapunzel,
Let down your golden hair!'

JAMES K. BAXTER

Johnnie Groat Says

Johnnie Groat says my eyes are blue,
He says my hair is curled,
He says I am the prettiest maid
He saw in all the world.

    Dearest, your hair is straight as string,
    One eye is black, one brown,
    And you are the homeliest-looking girl
    Was ever in Launceston town.

Johnnie Groat says I'm smart and slim,
My hands are soft as snow,
And nobody walks as well as I
When to the fields I go.

    Sweetheart, your shift is all in rags,
    Your hands are red as kale,
    And it's well-known at sixteen stone
    You turn the miller's scale.

Johnnie Groat says my voice is sweet
As water is or wine,
And when my grannie goes up to heaven
Her pig and cot are mine.

    Dear, when you walk about the wood
    The birds fall down on the floor,
    And your grannie of fifty years is good
    For half a century more.

Then shall I not marry good Johnnie Groat
Who thinks so well of me?
And shall he not give me a fine gold ring
When he goes back to sea?

Daughter, but take the fine gold ring
And the love that's in his eye,
For the love that comes from an honest poor man
Is more than money can buy,
More than money can buy.

CHARLES CAUSLEY

A Knight and a Lady

A knight and a lady
  Went riding one day
Far into the forest,
  Away, away.

'Fair knight,' said the lady,
  'I pray, have a care.
This forest is evil –
  Beware, beware!'

A fiery red dragon
  They spied on the grass;
The lady wept sorely,
  Alas! Alas!

The knight slew the dragon,
  The lady was gay.
They rode on together,
  Away, away.

ANON

Here lies Fred

Here lies Fred,
Who was alive and is dead:
Had it been his father,
I had much rather;
Had it been his brother,
Still better than another;
Had it been his sister,
No one would have missed her;
Had it been the whole generation,
So much the better for the nation:
But since 'tis only Fred,
Who was alive and is dead,
There's no more to be said.

ANON

On Martha Snell

Poor Martha Snell, she's gone away;
She would have stayed, but could not stay.
She had bad legs and a hacking cough;
It was her legs that carried her off.

ANON

On Stubborn Michael Shay

Here lies the body of Michael Shay,
Who died maintaining his right of way.
His case was clear and his will was strong —
But he's as dead as if he'd been wrong.

ANON

On John Bun

Here lies John Bun;
He was killed by a gun.
His name was not Bun, but Wood;
But Wood would not rhyme with gun, and Bun would.

ANON

The Animal Fair

I went to the animal fair;
The birds and the beasts were there;
The big baboon by the light of the moon
Was combing his auburn hair.

The monkey he got drunk
And sat on the elephant's trunk.
The elephant sneezed and fell on his knees,
And that was the end of the monkey-monk.

ANON

The Great Panjandrum Himself

So she went into the garden
to cut a cabbage-leaf
to make an apple-pie;
and at the same time
a great she-bear, coming from the street,
pops its head into the shop.
What! no soap?
So he died,
and she very imprudently married the Barber:
and there were present
the Picninnies,
and the Joblillies,
and the Garyulies,
and the great Panjandrum himself,
with the little round button at top;
and they all fell to playing the game
of catch-as-catch-can,
till the gunpowder ran out at the heels of their boots.

SAMUEL FOOTE

The Man in the Wilderness

The Man in the Wilderness asked of me
'How many blackberries grow in the sea?'
I answered him as I thought good,
'As many red herrings as grow in the wood.'

The Man in the Wilderness asked me why
His hen could swim, and his pig could fly.
I answered him briskly as I thought best,
'Because they were born in a cuckoo's nest.'

The Man in the Wilderness asked me to tell
The sands in the sea and I counted them well.
Says he with a grin, 'And not one more?'
I answered him bravely, 'You go and make sure!'

ANON

Jumper

When I was a lad as big as my Dad,
I jumped into a pea-pod;
Pea-pod was so full,
I jumped into a roaring bull;
Roaring bull was so fat,
I jumped into a gentleman's hat;
Gentleman's hat was so fine,
I jumped into a bottle of wine;
Bottle of wine was so clear,
I jumped into a bottle of beer;
Bottle of beer was so thick,
I jumped into a knobbed stick;
Knobbed stick wouldn't bend,
I jumped into a turkey hen;
Turkey hen wouldn't lay,
I jumped into a piece of clay;
Piece of clay was so nasty,
I jumped into an apple pasty;
Apple pasty was so good,
I jumped into a lump of wood;
Lump of wood was so rotten,
I jumped into a bale of cotton;
The bale of cotton set on fire,
Blew me up to Jeremiah;
Jeremiah was a prophet,
Had a horse and couldn't stop it;
Horse knocked against t'ould cobbler's door,
Knocked t'ould cobbler on the floor;
Cobbler with his rusty gun,
Shot the horse and off it run.

ANON

'Biby's' Epitaph

A muvver was barfin' 'er biby one night,
The youngest of ten and a tiny young mite,
The muvver was poor and the biby was thin,
Only a skelington covered in skin:
The muvver turned rahnd for the soap off the rack,
She was but a moment, but when she turned back,
The biby was gorn; and in anguish she cried,
'Oh, where is my biby?' – The angels replied:

'Your biby 'as fell dahn the plug-'ole,
Your biby 'as gorn dahn the plug;
The poor little thing was so skinny and thin
'E oughter been barfed in a jug;
Your biby is perfeckly 'appy,
'E won't need a barf any more,
Your biby 'as fell dahn the plug-'ole,
Not lorst, but gorn before.'

ANON

Algy

Algy met a bear,
A bear met Algy.
The bear was bulgy,
The bulge was Algy.

ANON

The Common Cormorant

The common cormorant or shag
Lays eggs inside a paper bag
The reason you will see no doubt
It is to keep the lightning out.
But what these unobservant birds
Have never noticed is that herds
Of wandering bears may come with buns
And steal the bags to hold the crumbs.

ANON

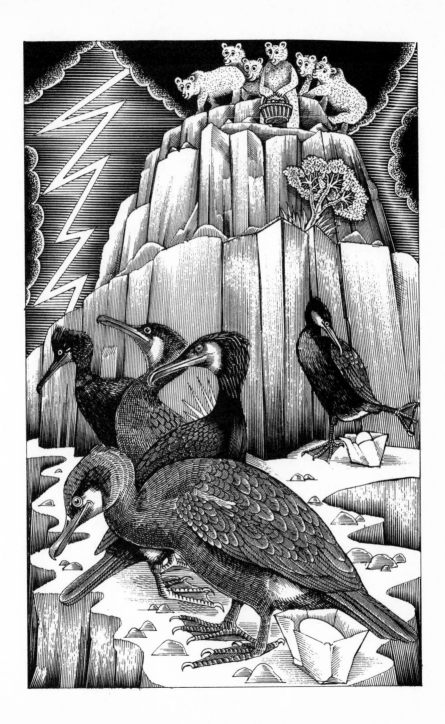

The Walloping Window-Blind

A capital ship for an ocean trip
  Was *The Walloping Window-Blind*;
No gale that blew dismayed her crew
  Or troubled the captain's mind.
The man at the wheel was taught to feel
  Contempt for the wildest blow,
And it often appeared, when the weather had cleared,
  That he'd been in his bunk below.

The boatswain's mate was very sedate,
  Yet fond of amusement, too;
And he played hop-scotch with the starboard watch
  While the captain tickled the crew.
And the gunner we had was apparently mad,
  For he sat on the after-rail,
And fired salutes with the captain's boots,
  In the teeth of the booming gale.

The captain sat in a commodore's hat,
  And dined, in a royal way,
On toasted pigs and pickles and figs
  And gummery bread, each day.
But the cook was Dutch, and behaved as such;
  For the food that he gave the crew
Was a number of tons of hot-cross buns,
  Chopped up with sugar and glue.

And we all felt ill as mariners will,
  On a diet that's cheap and rude;
And we shivered and shook as we dipped the cook
  In a tub of his gluesome food.
Then nautical pride we laid aside,
  And we cast the vessel ashore
On the Gulliby Isles, where the Poohpooh smiles,
  And the Anagazanders roar.

Composed of sand was that favoured land,
  And trimmed with cinnamon straws;
And pink and blue was the pleasing hue
  Of the Tickletoeteaser's claws.
And we sat on the edge of a sandy ledge
  And shot at the whistling bee;
And the Binnacle-bats wore water-proof hats
  As they danced in the sounding sea.

On rubagrub bark, from dawn to dark,
  We fed, till we all had grown
Uncommonly shrunk – when a Chinese junk
  Came by from the torriby zone.
She was stubby and square, but we didn't much care,
  And we cheerily put to sea;
And we left the crew of the junk to chew
  The bark of the rubagrub tree.

CHARLES EDWARD CARRYL

Calico Pie

Calico Pie,
The little Birds fly
Down to the calico tree,
 Their wings were blue,
 And they sang 'Tilly-loo!'
Till away they flew,—
  And they never came back to me!
   They never came back!
   They never came back!
  They never came back to me!

Calico Jam,
The little Fish swam,
Over the syllabub sea,
 He took off his hat,
 To the Sole and the Sprat,
And the Willeby-wat,—
  But he never came back to me!
   He never came back!
   He never came back!
  He never came back to me!

Calico Ban,
The little Mice ran,
To be ready in time for tea,
 Flippity flup,
 They drank it all up,
And danced in the cup,—

But they never came back to me!
They never came back!
They never came back!
They never came back to me!

Calico Drum,
The Grasshoppers come,
The Butterfly, Beetle, and Bee,
Over the ground,
Around and round,
With a hop and a bound,—
But they never came back!
They never came back!
They never came back!
They never came back to me!

EDWARD LEAR

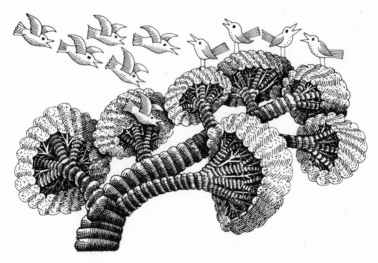

Derby Ram

As I was going to Derby, Sir, 'twas on a summer's day,
I met the finest ram, Sir, that ever was fed on hay,

And indeed, Sir, 'tis true, Sir, I never was given to lie,
And if you'd been to Derby, Sir, you'd have seen him
  as well as I.

It had four feet to walk on, Sir, it had four feet to stand,
And every foot it had, Sir, did cover an acre of land.

And indeed, Sir, 'tis true, Sir, I never was given to lie,
And if you'd been to Derby, Sir, you'd have seen him
  as well as I.

This ram it had a horn, Sir, that reached up to the sky,
The birds went up and built their nests, could hear the
  young ones cry.

And indeed, Sir, 'tis true, Sir, I never was given to lie,
And if you'd been to Derby, Sir, you'd have seen him
  as well as I.

This ram he had another horn that reached up to the moon,
The birds went up in January and didn't come down till June.

And indeed, Sir, 'tis true, Sir, I never was given to lie,
And if you'd been to Derby, Sir, you'd have seen him
  as well as I.

And all the men of Derby, Sir, came begging for his tail
To ring St George's passing-bell at the top of Derby jail.

And indeed, Sir, 'tis true, Sir, I never was given to lie,
And if you'd been to Derby, Sir, you'd have seen him
  as well as I.

And all the women of Derby, Sir, came begging for his ears
To make them leather aprons to last them forty years.

And indeed, Sir, 'tis true, Sir, I never was given to lie,
And if you'd been to Derby, Sir, you'd have seen him
  as well as I.

And all the boys of Derby, Sir, came begging for his eyes
To make a pair of footballs, for they were just the size.

And indeed, Sir, 'tis true, Sir, I never was given to lie,
And if you'd been to Derby, Sir, you'd have seen him
  as well as I.

The butcher that killed this ram, Sir, was in danger of his life,
He was up to his knees in blood crying out for a longer knife.

And indeed, Sir, 'tis true, Sir, I never was given to lie,
And if you'd been to Derby, Sir, you'd have seen him
  as well as I.

And now my song is ended, I have no more to say,
So please will you give us a New Year's gift, and let
  us go away.

And indeed, Sir, 'tis true, Sir, I never was given to lie
And if you'd been to Derby, Sir, you'd have seen him
  as well as I.

TRADITIONAL

Frog Went A-Courtin'

Mr. Froggie went a-courtin' an' he did ride;
Sword and pistol by his side.

He went to Missus Mousie's hall,
Gave a loud knock and gave a loud call.

'Pray, Missus Mousie, air you within?'
'Yes, kind sir, I set an' spin.'

He tuk Miss Mousie on his knee,
An' sez, 'Miss Mousie, will ya marry me?'

Miss Mousie blushed an' hung her head,
'You'll have t'ask Uncle Rat,' she said.

'Not without Uncle Rat's consent
Would I marry the Pres-i-dent.'

Uncle Rat jump up an' shuck his fat side,
To think his niece would be Bill Frog's bride.

Nex' day Uncle Rat went to town.
To git his niece a weddin' gown.

Whar shall the weddin' supper be?
'Way down yander in a holler tree.

First come in was a Bumble-bee,
Who danced a jig with Captain Flea.

Next come in was a Butterfly,
Sellin' butter very high.

An' when they all set down to sup,
A big grey goose come an' gobbled 'em all up.

An' this is the end of one, two, three,
The Rat an' the Mouse an' the little Froggie.

TRADITIONAL

Do your ears hang low?

Do your ears hang low?
Do they wobble to and fro?
Can you tie them in a knot?
Can you tie them in a bow?
Can you toss them over your shoulder
Like a regimental soldier?
Do your ears hang low?

TRADITIONAL

Linstead Market

Carry me ackie, go a Linstead market,
Not a quattie would sell.
Carry me ackie, go a Linstead market,
Not a quattie would sell.

  Lord, not a mite, not a bite,
  What a Saturday night!
  Lord, not a mite, not a bite,
  What a Saturday night!

Everybody come and feel them, feel them,
Not a quattie would sell.
Everybody come and feel them, feel them,
Not a quattie would sell.

Hear me call louder, ackie, ackie,
Red and pretty dem tan,
Come buy them for your Sunday morning breakfast,
Rice and ackie am grand.

See all the children come a-linga ling
For what their Mommy no bring.
See all the children come a-linga ling
For what their Mommy no bring.

TRADITIONAL

Any old iron?

Any old iron, any old iron,
Any any old, old iron?
You look neat, talk about a treat,
You look dapper from your napper
  to your feet.
Dressed in style, brand new tile,
And your father's old green tie on,
But I wouldn't give you tuppence for your
  old watch chain,
Old iron, old iron?

Ta-da-la-la-la-la,
Ta-da-la-la-la-la,
I tiddly-i-ti,
Pom, pom!

TRADITIONAL

Dogs

I am his Highness' dog at Kew.
Pray tell me sir – whose dog are you?

ALEXANDER POPE

'Progress'

I AM a sundial, and I make a botch
Of what is done far better by a watch.

HILAIRE BELLOC

A Horse and a Flea

A horse and a flea and three blind mice
Sat on a kerbstone shooting dice.
The horse he slipped and fell on the flea.
The flea said, 'Whoops, there's a horse on me.'

ANON

Swan Song

Swans sing before they die – 'twere no bad thing
Should certain persons die before they sing.

SAMUEL TAYLOR COLERIDGE

I Sometimes Think

I sometimes think I'd rather crow
And be a rooster than to roost
And be a crow. But I dunno.

A rooster he can roost also,
Which don't seem fair when crows can't crow.
Which may help some. Still I dunno.

Crows should be glad of one thing, though;
Nobody thinks of eating crow,
While roosters they are good enough
For anyone unless they're tough.

There are lots of tough old roosters though,
And anyway a crow can't crow,
So mebby roosters stand more show.
It looks that way. But I dunno.

ANON

Goldfish

the scene of the crime
was a goldfish bowl
goldfish were kept
in the bowl at the time:

that was the scene
and that was the crime

ALAN JACKSON

Chinchilla

Chinchillas now are all protected
Against the furriers, who, dejected,
Have to do their level best to
Make fur coats of polyester;
Although they know this, there is still a
Wariness in each chinchilla.

MARJORIE BAKER

The Frog

What a wonderful bird the frog are –
When he sit, he stand almost;
When he hop, he fly almost.
He ain't got no sense hardly;
He ain't got no tail hardly either.
When he sit, he sit on what he ain't got – almost.

ANON

I Like to Stay Up

I like to stay up
and listen
when big people talking
jumbie stories

I does feel
so tingly and excited
inside me

But when my mother say
'Girl, time for bed'

Then is when
I does feel a dread

Then is when
I does jump into me bed

Then is when
I does cover up
from me feet to me head

Then is when
I does wish I didn't listen
to no stupid jumbie story

Then is when
I does wish I did read
me book instead

GRACE NICHOLS
'Jumbie' is a Guyanese word for 'ghost'

Charm Against an Egg-Boat

There's an old superstition that says that if you eat a boiled egg you must smash the shell up quickly to stop the witches stealing the unbroken shells, turning them into boats and rowing out to sea to brew up storms.

You must break the shell to bits, for fear
The witches should make it a boat, my dear:
For over the sea, away from home,
Far by night the witches roam.

ANON

'The Soul is the Breath
in Your Body'

You can sell them for a penny to
your mother

                                                    or

You can tie knots for each one
in a piece of string
and plant it at the bottom of your garden
and water it
every morning
that makes them grow under the earth

                                                    or

You can have them charmed
if you know a charmer
there are lots in Cornwall you must
leave her a gift and not say thankyou
then she will sing
an incantation

                                                    or

there is the witches way.
You take a special white round stone
for every one
and put them in a pretty red bag
throw it over your shoulder
into the middle of the road –

*Don't touch that bag it's got
warts in it*

                                                    or

If you can find the green toad you
got them from you can
give them back to him if he'll have them

or

You can rub snails on them or slugs
and if that doesn't cure them
you still want them

JENI COUZYN

What Was It?

What was it
that could make
me wake
in the middle of the night
when the light
was a long way from coming
and the humming
of the fridge was the single
tingle
of sound
all round?

Why, when I crept downstairs and watched
green numbers sprinting on the kitchen clock,
was I afraid the empty rocking chair
might start to rock?

Why, when I stole back up and heard
the creak of each stair to my own
heart's quickening beats,

was I afraid that I should find
some other thing from the night outside
between my sheets?

KIT WRIGHT

Have You Seen the Hidebehind?

Have you seen the Hidebehind?
I don't think you will, mind you,
because as you're running through the dark
the Hidebehind's behind you.

MICHAEL ROSEN

Anancy

Anancy is a spider;
Anancy is a man;
Anancy's West Indian
And West African.

Sometimes, he wears a waistcoat;
Sometimes, he carries a cane;
Sometimes, he sports a top hat;
Sometimes, he's just a plain,
Ordinary, black, hairy spider.

Anancy is vastly cunning,
Tremendously greedy,
Excessively charming,
Hopelessly dishonest,
Warmly loving,
Firmly confident,
Fiercely wild,
A fabulous character,
Completely out of our mind
And out of his, too.

Anancy is a master planner,
A great user
Of other people's plans;
He pockets everybody's food,
Shelter, land, money, and more;
He achieves mountains of things,
Like stolen flour dumplings;
He deceives millions of people,
Even the man in the moon;
And he solves all the mysteries
On earth, in air, under sea.

And always,
Anancy changes
From a spider into a man
And from a man into a spider
And back again
At the drop of a sleepy eyelid.

ANDREW SALKEY

Granny Granny
Please Comb my Hair

Granny Granny please comb
my hair
you always take your time
you always take such care

You put me on a cushion
between your knees
you rub a little coconut oil
parting gentle as a breeze

Mummy Mummy
she's always in a hurry-hurry
rush
she pulls my hair
sometimes she tugs

But Granny
you have all the time
in the world
and when you're finished
you always turn my head and say
'Now who's a nice girl'

GRACE NICHOLS

The Fox Rhyme

Aunt was on the garden seat
  Enjoying a wee nap and
Along came a fox! teeth
  Closed with a snap and
He's running to the woods with her
  A-dangle and a-flap and –
Run, uncle, run
  And see what has happened!

IAN SERRAILLIER

Daddy Fell into the Pond

Everyone grumbled. The sky was grey.
We had nothing to do and nothing to say.
We were nearing the end of a dismal day,
And there seemed to be nothing beyond,
                    THEN
        Daddy fell into the pond!

And everyone's face grew merry and bright,
And Timothy danced for sheer delight.
'Give me the camera, quick, oh quick!
He's crawling out of the duckweed.' *Click!*

Then the gardener suddenly slapped his knee,
And he doubled up, shaking silently,
And the ducks all quacked as if they were daft
And it sounded as if the old drake laughed.

O, there wasn't a thing that didn't respond
                    WHEN
        Daddy fell into the pond!

                                    ALFRED NOYES

Ducklings

Here I am the stranger
foreign in a foreign land
standing in a sun-cracked red dirt yard
back home for Mum and Dad
a thousand miles from home for me

The landscape like a mixed up dream
the farm perched high above
deep bitten valleys and
in a distant circle limestone cliffs
a hundred miles from sea
And here I am
feeding Uncle's ducklings
who gobble gobble gobble
every scrap of corn I throw them
scrambling over hard baked cart ruts
climbing over fallen brothers
rushing headlong to get
big and fat
just how Uncle wants them

Laughing from the doorway
behind – the flagstoned kitchen
shuttered cool and dark

a glass of wine held out to me
everybody's waiting and
I've been forgiven

my soft and stupid yesterday
Poor little English
too tender of heart to eat
the slab of coarse fat
duck's liver pâté
home made

for the foreigner
so foolish rude and clumsy
standing in a red dirt yard
a thousand miles from home

MICK GOWAR

Idyll

I knew a child called Alma Brent,
  Completely destitute of brains,
Whose principal accomplishment
Was imitating railway trains.

When ladies called at 'Sunnyside',
Mama, to keep the party clean,
Would say, with pardonable pride,
  'Now, Alma, do the six-fifteen.'

The child would grunt and snort and puff,
With weird contortions of the face,
And when the guests had had enough,
She'd cease, with one last wild grimace.

One day her jovial Uncle Paul
  Cried, 'Come on, Alma! Do your worst!'
And, challenged thus before them all,
  She did the four-nineteen – and burst.

J.B. MORTON

Happy Birthday, Dilroy!

My name is Dilroy.
I'm a little black boy
and I'm eight today.

My birthday cards say
it's great to be eight
and they sure right
coz I got a pair of skates
I want for a long time.

My birthday cards say,
Happy Birthday, Dilroy!
But, Mummy, tell me why
they don't put a little boy
that looks a bit like me.
Why the boy on the card so white?

JOHN AGARD

I Share my Bedroom

I share my bedroom with my brother
and I don't like it.
His bed's by the window
under my map of England's railways
that has a hole in just above Leicester
where Tony Sanders, he says,
killed a Roman centurion
with the Radio Times.

My bed's in the corner
and the paint on the skirting board
wrinkles when I push it with my thumb
which I do sometimes when I go to bed
sometimes when I wake up
but mostly on Sundays
when we stay in bed all morning.

That's when he makes pillow dens
under the blankets
so that only his left eye shows
and when I go deep-bed mining
for elastoplast spools
that I scatter with my feet
the night before,
and I jump on to his bed
shouting: eeyoueeyoueeyouee
heaping pillows on his head:
'Now breathe, now breathe'
and then there's quiet and silence
so I pull it away quick
and he's there laughing all over
sucking fresh air along his breathing-tube fingers.

Actually, sharing's all right.

MICHAEL ROSEN

The Dancing Cabman

Alone on the lawn
  The cabman dances;
In the dew of the dawn
  He kicks and prances.
His bowler is set
  On his bullet-head.
For his boots are wet
  And his aunt is dead.
There on the lawn
  As the light advances,
On the tide of the dawn,
  The cabman dances.

Swift and strong
  As a garden roller,
He dances along
  In his little bowler,

Skimming the lawn
  With royal grace,
The dew of the dawn
  On his great red face.
To fairy flutes,
  As the light advances,
In square, black boots
  The cabman dances.

J.B. MORTON

My Dad's Thumb

My dad's thumb
can stick pins in wood
without flinching –
it can crush family-size matchboxes
in one stroke
and lever off jam-jar lids without piercing
at the pierce here sign.

If it wanted
it could be a bath-plug
or a paint-scraper
a keyhole cover or a tap-tightener.

It's already a great nutcracker
and if it dressed up
it could easily pass
as a broad bean or a big toe.

In actual fact, it's quite simply
the world's fastest envelope burster.

MICHAEL ROSEN

from *Aunts and Uncles*

When Aunty Jane
Became a Crane
She put one leg behind her head;
And even when the clock struck ten
Refused to go to bed.

When Aunty Grace
Became a Plaice
She all but vanished sideways on;
Except her nose
And pointed toes
The rest of her was gone.

When Aunty Jill
Became a Pill
She stared all day through dark-blue glass;
And always sneered
When men appeared
To ask her how she was.

When Uncle Jake
Became a Snake
He never found it out;
And so as no one mentions it
One sees him still about.

MERVYN PEAKE

My Uncle Dan

My Uncle Dan's an inventor, you may think that's
       very fine.
You may wish he was your Uncle instead of being mine –
If he wanted he could make a watch that bounces
       when it drops,
He could make a helicopter out of string and bottle tops
Or any really useful thing you can't get in the shops.
But Uncle Dan has other ideas:
The bottomless glass for ginger beers,
The toothless saw that's safe for the tree,
A special word for a spelling bee
(Like Lionocerangoutangadder),
Or the roll-uppable rubber ladder,
The mystery pie that bites when it's bit –
My Uncle Dan invented it.
My Uncle Dan sits in his den inventing night and day.
His eyes peer from his hair and beard like mice
       from a load of hay.
And does he make the shoes that will go walks
       without your feet?
A shrinker to shrink instantly the elephants you meet?
A carver that just carves from the air steaks
       cooked and ready to eat?
No, no, he has other intentions –
Only perfectly useless inventions:
Glassless windows (they never break),
A medicine to cure the earthquake,
The unspillable screwed-down cup,
The stairs that go neither down nor up,
The door you simply paint on a wall –
Uncle Dan invented them all.

TED HUGHES

Sir Smasham Uppe

Good afternoon, Sir Smasham Uppe!
We're having tea: do take a cup!
Sugar and milk? Now let me see –
Two lumps, I think? . . . Good gracious me!
The silly thing slipped off your knee!
Pray don't apologize, old chap:
A very trivial mishap!
So clumsy of you? How absurd!
My dear Sir Smasham, not a word!
Now do sit down and have another,
And tell us all about your brother –
You know, the one who broke his head.
Is the poor fellow still in bed? –
A chair – allow me, sir! . . . Great Scott!
That *was* a nasty smash! Eh, what?
Oh, not at all: the chair was old –
Queen Anne, or so we have been told.
We've got at least a dozen more:
Just leave the pieces on the floor.
I want you to admire our view;
Come nearer to the window, do;
And look how beautiful . . . Tut, tut!
You didn't see that it was shut?
I hope you are not badly cut!
Not hurt? A fortunate escape!
Amazing! Not a single scrape!

And now, if you have finished tea,
I fancy you might like to see
A little thing or two I've got.
That china plate? Yes, worth a lot:
A beauty too ... Ah, there it goes!
I trust it didn't hurt your toes?
Your elbow brushed it off the shelf?
Of course: I've done the same myself.
And now, my dear Sir Smasham – Oh,
You surely don't intend to go?
You *must* be off? Well, come again.
So glad you're fond of porcelain!

E.V. RIEU

Little Clotilda

Little Clotilda,
Well and hearty,
Thought she'd like
To give a party.
But as her friends
Were shy and wary,
Nobody came
But her own canary.

ANON

Wha Me Mudder Do

Mek me tell you wha me Mudder do
wha me mudder do
wha me mudder do

Me mudder pound plantain mek fufu
Me mudder catch crab mek calaloo stew

Mek me tell you wha me mudder do
wha me mudder do
wha me mudder do

Me mudder beat hammer
Me mudder turn screw
she paint chair red
then she paint it blue

Mek me tell you wha me mudder do
wha me mudder do
wha me mudder do

Me mudder chase bad-cow
with one 'Shoo'
she paddle down river
in she own canoe
Ain't have nothing
dat me mudder can't do
Ain't have nothing
dat me mudder can't do

Mek me tell you

GRACE NICHOLS

Full Moon Rhyme

There's a hare in the moon tonight,
crouching alone in the bright
buttercup field of the moon;
and all the dogs in the world
howl at the hare in the moon.

'I chased that hare to the sky,'
the hungry dogs all cry.
'The hare jumped into the moon
and left me here in the cold.
I chased that hare to the moon.'

'Come down again, mad hare,
we can see you there,'
the dogs all howl to the moon.
'Come down again to the world,
you mad black hare in the moon,

or we will grow wings and fly
up to the star-grassed sky
to hunt you out of the moon,'
the hungry dogs of the world
howl at the hare in the moon.

JUDITH WRIGHT

Escape at Bedtime

THE lights from the parlour and kitchen shone out
   Through the blinds and the windows and bars;
And high overhead and all moving about,
   There were thousands of millions of stars.
There ne'er were such thousands of leaves on a tree,
   Nor of people in church or the Park,
As the crowds of the stars that looked down upon me,
   And that glittered and winked in the dark.

The Dog, and the Plough, and the Hunter, and all,
   And the star of the sailor, and Mars,
These shone in the sky, and the pail by the wall
   Would be half full of water and stars.
They saw me at last, and they chased me with cries,
   And they soon had me packed into bed;
But the glory kept shining and bright in my eyes,
   And the stars going round in my head.

ROBERT LOUIS STEVENSON

The Night will Never Stay

THE night will never stay,
The night will still go by,
Though with a million stars
You pin it to the sky;
Though you bind it with the blowing wind
And buckle it with the moon,
The night will slip away
Like sorrow or a tune.

ELEANOR FARJEON

Full of the Moon

It's full of the moon
The dogs dance out
Through brush and bush and bramble.
They howl and yowl
And growl and prowl.
They amble, ramble, scramble.
They rush through brush.
They push through bush.
They yip and yap and hurr.
They lark around and bark around
With prickles in their fur.
They two-step in the meadow.
They polka on the lawn.
Tonight's the night
The dogs dance out
And chase their tails till dawn.

KARLA KUSKIN

In Quiet Night

In quiet night
the horns honking up from the street
make mad voices
to other horns, tyres shriek
to other tyres, brakes shriek
to other brakes.

Somewhere, there is a night of trees,
of great, bulging bullfrogs croaking
in ponds. Screech owls cry to a forest
of birds
    shrieking.

Horns, in quiet night, honk up songs
no frog, no bird, has ever sung.

MYRA COHN LIVINGSTON

The Tide in the River

The tide in the river,
The tide in the river,
The tide in the river runs deep.
  I saw a shiver
  Pass over the river
As the tide turned in its sleep.

ELEANOR FARJEON

Lullaby

Sh sh what do you wish
sh sh the windows are shuttered
sh sh a magical fish
swims out from the window and down to the river

lap lap the waters are lapping
sh sh the shore slips away
glide glide glide with the current
sh sh the shadows are deeper

sleep sleep tomorrow is sure

EVE MERRIAM

Hare

Midsummer madness
And the March hare
Galloping across fields
With nowhere to go but home
And happy for it.

ADELE DAVIDE

A Narrow Fellow in the Grass

A narrow fellow in the grass
Occasionally rides;
You may have met him, – did you not?
His notice sudden is.

The grass divides as with a comb,
A spotted shaft is seen;
And then it closes at your feet
And opens further on.

He likes a boggy acre,
A floor too cool for corn.
Yet when a child, and barefoot,
I more than once, at morn,

Have passed, I thought, a whip-lash
Unbraiding in the sun, –
When, stooping to secure it,
It wrinkled, and was gone.

Several of nature's people
I know, and they know me;
I feel for them a transport
Of cordiality;

But never met this fellow,
Attended or alone,
Without a tighter breathing,
And zero at the bone.

EMILY DICKINSON

Marjory Fleming was born in 1803 and died a few weeks before her ninth birthday. She kept a diary as soon as she could write and composed many poems. Here are two of them.

To a Monkey

O lovely O most charming pug
Thy gracefull air and heavenly mug
The beauties of his mind do shine
And every bit is shaped so fine
Your very tail is most devine
Your teeth is whiter than the snow
You are a great buck and a bow
Your eyes are of so fine a shape
More like a christains than an ape
His cheeks is like the roses blume
Your hair is like the ravens plume
His noses cast is of the roman
He is a very pretty weoman
I could not get a rhyme for roman
And was oblidged to call it weoman.

MARJORY FLEMING

A Melancholy Lay

Three Turkeys fair their last have breathed,
And now this world for ever leaved,
Their Father and their Mother too,
Will sigh and weep as well as you,
Mourning for their offspring fair,
Whom they did nurse with tender care.
Indeed the rats their bones have crunch'd,
To eternity are they launch'd;
Their graceful form and pretty eyes
Their fellow fowls did not despise,
A direful death indeed they had,
That would put any parent mad,
But she was more than usual calm
She did not give a single dam.
Here ends this melancholy lay:
Farewell poor Turkeys I must say.

MARJORY FLEMING

Four Things

There be four things which are little upon the earth,
but they are exceeding wise:

The ants are a people not strong,
yet they prepare their meat in the summer;

The conies are but a feeble folk,
yet they make their houses in the rocks;

The locusts have no king,
yet go they forth all of them by bands.

The spider taketh hold with her hands,
and is in kings' palaces.

THE BIBLE: PROVERBS, 30

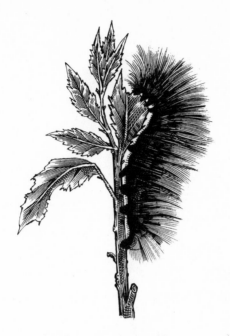

The Caterpillar

Brown and furry
Caterpillar in a hurry;
Take your walk
To the shady leaf or stalk.

May no toad spy you,
May the little birds pass by you;
Spin and die,
To live again a butterfly.

CHRISTINA ROSSETTI

Five Eyes

In Hans' old mill his three black cats
Watch his bins for the thieving rats.
Whisker and claw, they crouch in the night,
Their five eyes smouldering green and bright:
Squeaks from the flour sacks, squeaks from where
The cold wind stirs on the empty stair,
Squeaking and scampering, everywhere.
Then down they pounce, now in, now out,
At whisking tail, and sniffing snout;
While lean old Hans he snores away
Till peep of light at break of day;
Then up he climbs to his creaking mill,
Out come his cats all grey with meal –
Jekkel, and Jessup, and one-eyed Jill.

WALTER DE LA MARE

He Was a Rat

He was a rat, and she was a rat,
  And down in one hole they did dwell,
And both were as black as a witch's cat,
  And they loved each other well.

He had a tail, and she had a tail,
  Both long and curling and fine;
And each said, 'Yours is the finest tail
  In the world, excepting mine.'

He smelt the cheese, and she smelt the cheese,
  And they both pronounced it good;
And both remarked it would greatly add
  To the charms of their daily food.

So he ventured out, and she ventured out,
  And I saw them go with pain;
But what befell them I never can tell,
  For they never came back again.

ANON

The Donkey

I saw a donkey
One day old,
His head was too big
For his neck to hold;
His legs were shaky
And long and loose,
They rocked and staggered
And weren't much use.

He tried to gambol
And frisk a bit,
But he wasn't quite sure
Of the trick of it.
His queer little coat
Was soft and grey,
And curled at his neck
In a lovely way.

His face was wistful
And left no doubt
That he felt life needed
Some thinking about.
So he blundered round
In venturesome quest,
And then lay flat
On the ground to rest.

He looked so little
And weak and slim,
I prayed the world
Might be good to him.

ANON

The Donkey

When fishes flew and forests walked
   And figs grew upon thorn,
Some moment when the moon was blood
   Then surely I was born.

With monstrous head and sickening cry
   And ears like errant wings,
The devil's walking parody
   On all four-footed things.

The tattered outlaw of the earth,
   Of ancient crooked will,
Starve, scourge, deride me: I am dumb,
   I keep my secret still.

Fools! For I also had my hour;
   One far fierce hour and sweet:
There was a shout about my ears,
   And palms before my feet.

G.K. CHESTERTON

Cat

Cat!
Scat!
Atter her, atter her,
Sleeky flatterer,
Spitfire chatterer,
Scatter her, scatter her,
    Off her mat!
    Wuff!
    Wuff!
    Treat her rough!
Git her, git her,
Whiskery spitter!
Catch her, catch her,
Green-eyed scratcher!
    Slathery
    Slithery
    Hisser,
    Don't miss her!

Run till you're dithery,
    Hithery
    Thithery
    Pfitts! Pfitts!
    How she spits!
    Spitch! Spatch!
    Can't she scratch!

Scritching the bark
Of the sycamore-tree,
She's reached her ark
And's hissing at me
Pfitts! Pfitts!
Wuff! Wuff!
Scat,
Cat!
That's
That!

ELEANOR FARJEON

Cat's Funeral

Bury her deep, down deep,
Safe in the earth's cold keep,
Bury her deep –

No more to watch bird stir;
No more to clean dark fur;
No more to glisten as silk;
No more to revel in milk;
No more to purr.

Bury her deep, down deep;
She is beyond warm sleep.
She will not walk in the night;
She will not wake to the light.
Bury her deep.

E.V. RIEU

Mole

To have to be a mole?

It is like, in a way,
being a little car driven
in the very dark,
                    owned
by these endless-
ly tunnelling paws and small
eyes that are good, only,
for the underground.

What can you know of me, this
warm black engine of
busying velvet?

Soft mounds of new, pale
earth like finely-flaked ash
tell you just about where
my country is, but
do you ever see
                    me?

ALAN BROWNJOHN

Upon the Snail

She goes but softly, but she goeth sure;
  She stumbles not as stronger creatures do:
Her journey's shorter, so she may endure
  Better than they which do much further go.

She makes no noise, but stilly seizeth on
  The flower or herb appointed for her food,
The which she quietly doth feed upon,
  While others range, and gare, but find no good.

And though she doth but very softly go,
  However 'tis not fast, nor slow, but sure;
And certainly they that do travel so,
  The prize they do aim at, they do procure.

JOHN BUNYAN

Gare means to stare about

The Tyger

Tyger! Tyger! burning bright
In the forests of the night,
What immortal hand or eye
Could frame thy fearful symmetry?

In what distant deeps or skies
Burnt the fire of thine eyes?
On what wings dare he aspire?
What the hand dare seize the fire?

And what shoulder, & what art,
Could twist the sinews of thy heart?
And when thy heart began to beat,
What dread hand? & what dread feet?

What the hammer? what the chain?
In what furnace was thy brain?
What the anvil? what dread grasp
Dare its deadly terrors clasp?

When the stars threw down their spears,
And water'd heaven with their tears,
Did he smile his work to see?
Did he who made the Lamb make thee?
Tyger! Tyger! burning bright
In the forests of the night,
What immortal hand or eye,
Dare frame thy fearful symmetry?

WILLIAM BLAKE

Special thanks are due to Charles Causley for permission to use a quotation from *I am the Song* as the title to this book.

The author and publishers gratefully acknowledge permission to reprint the following poems in this book:

JOHN AGARD, *Happy Birthday, Dilroy*, from *I Din Do Nuttin*, illus. Susanna Gretz, The Bodley Head; MARJORIE BAKER, *Chinchilla*, © Marjorie Baker; JAMES K. BAXTER, *Rapunzel* and *The Firemen*, from *The Treehouse* by permission of Mrs J. C. Baxter and Price Milburn & Co Ltd; HILAIRE BELLOC, *Progress*, by permission of Gerald Duckworth & Co Ltd and the Peters Fraser & Dunlop Group Ltd; DIONNE BRAND, *Wind*, © Dionne Brand; ALAN BROWNJOHN, *Mole*, © Alan Brownjohn; CHARLES CAUSLEY, *I am the Song, Early in the Morning*, from *Early in the Morning; Johnnie Groat Says*, from *Figgie Hobbin*, Viking Kestrel, by permission of David Higham Assoc; MYRA COHN LIVINGSTON, *In Quiet Night*, from *A Song I Sang to You*, Copyright © 1958, 1959, 1965, 1967, 1969 1984 by Myra Cohn Livingston. All rights reserved. By permission of Marian Reiner for the author; JENI COUZYN, *The Soul is the Breath in Your Body*, © Jeni Couzyn; E. E, CUMMINGS, *maggie and milly and molly and may*, from *Complete Poems* 1913-1962, by permission of Liveright Publishing Corporation and Grafton Books, Copyright ©1923,1925,1931,1935, 1938,1939,1940,1944,1945,1946,1947,1948 1949,1950,1951,1952,1953, 1954,1955,1956,1957,1958,1959,1960,1961,1962, by the Trustees for the E.E. Cummings Trust. Copyright © 1961, 1963, 1968 by Marion Morehouse Cummings; ADELE DAVIDE, *Hare*, © Adele Davide from *A Footprint on the Air*, compiled Naomi Lewis, Hutchinson, 1983; WALTER DE LA MARE, *Five Eyes*, by permission of the Literary Trustees of Walter de la Mare and The Society of Authors as their representative; OLIVE DOVE, *Write a Poem*, © Olive Dove; ELEANOR FARJEON, *Cat, The Tide in the River, The Night will never Stay*, Michael Joseph, by permission of David Higham Assoc.; MICK GOWAR, *Ducklings* from *Swings and Roundabouts*, © Mick Gowar, Collins; ROBERT GRAVES, *The Penny Fiddle*, by permission of A.P. Watt Ltd, on behalf of the Executors of the Estate of Robert Graves; RUSSELL HOBAN, *London City*, from *The Pedalling Man* ©1968 by Russell Hoban by permission of William Heinemann Ltd; and Harold

Ober Associates Inc; RALPH HODGSON, *Stupidity Street*, from *Poems*, by permission of Mrs Hodgson and Macmillan, London and Basingstoke, and Macmillan Publishing Company, Copyright 1917 by Macmillan Publishing Company, renewed 1945 by Ralph Hodgson; MIROSLAV HOLUB, *The Door*, from selected poems of Miroslav Holub, translated by Ian Milner and George Theiner, © Miroslav Holub 1967, translation © Penguin Books 1967; TED HUGHES, *My Uncle Dan*, from *Meet My Folks*; *Foxgloves*, from *Moon-Whales*, by permission of Faber and Faber Ltd; ALAN JACKSON, *Goldfish*, © Alan Jackson; KARLA KUSKIN, *Full of the Moon*, from *Dogs and Dragons, Trees and Dreams*, Copyright © 1958 by Karla Kuskin, by permission of Harper & Row, Publishers, Inc; C. S. LEWIS from *The Dragon Speaks*, Collins Fount; ROGER McGOUGH, *First Day at School*, from *In the Glassroom*, Jonathan Cape and the Peters, Fraser & Dunlop Group Ltd, *The Writer of this Poem* from *Sky in the Pie*, by permission of the Peters, Fraser & Dunlop Group Ltd; EVE MERRIAM, *Mean Song, Lullaby, Weather*, from *Jamboree Rhymes for all Times*, Copyright © 1962,1964,1966,1973,1984, by Eve Merriam. All rights reserved. By permission of Marian Reiner for the author; J.B. MORTON, *The Dancing Cabman*, Century Hutchinson Ltd, *Idyll*, from *The Best of Beachcomber*, © Express Newspapers plc; GRACE NICHOLS, *I Like to Stay Up, My Hair, Wha Me Mudder Do?* from *Come on into my Tropical Garden*, A. & C. Black, © Grace Nichols 1984, by permission of Curtis Brown Group Ltd; ALFRED NOYES, *Daddy Fell into the Pond*, from *Collected Poems of Alfred Noyes*, by permission of John Murray (Publishers) Ltd and Hugh Noyes, Executor; GARETH OWEN, *Salford Road*, from *Salford Road*, © Gareth Owen, Kestrel Books 1979, by permission of Rogers, Coleridge & White Ltd; MERVYN PEAKE from *Aunts and Uncles*, from *A Book of Nonsense* by Mervyn Peake, Peter Owen, London; SYLVIA PLATH, *Mushrooms*, from *The Colossus*, Faber and Faber Ltd, and *The Collected Poems*, Harper & Row, Publishers, Inc., Copyright © Ted Hughes 1960, 1965, 1967, 1971, 1981, by permission of Olwyn Hughes and Harper & Row, Publishers, Inc.; JAMES REEVES, *The Sea*, from *The Wandering Moon and Other Poems*, Puffin Books, by permission of Laura Cecil Agency on behalf of the Estate of James Reeves; E.V. RIEU, *The Cat's Funeral, The Paint Box*, from *A Puffin Quartet of Modern Poets*, *Sir Smasham Uppe*, from *Cuckoo Calling*, Methuen, by permission of Richard Rieu, Executor; MICHAEL ROSEN, *My Dad's Thumb, Have you seen the Hidebehind? I Share my Bedroom...*, from *Mind Your Own Business*, © Michael Rosen 1974, Andre Deutsch Ltd; ANDREW SALKEY, *Anancy*, © Andrew Salkey; VERNON SCANNELL, *Poem on Bread*, © Vernon Scannell; E. J. SCOVELL, *The Boy Fishing*, from *Collected Poems*, Carcanet Press Ltd; IAN SERRAILLIER, *The Fox Rhyme*, © 1950 Ian Serraillier, Oxford University Press; MAY SWENSON, *Cat and the Weather*, Copyright © 1963 by May Swenson, by permission of the author; JUDITH WRIGHT, *Full Moon Rhyme*, from *Selected Poems: Five Senses* by Judith Wright, by permission of Angus & Robertson (UK); KIT WRIGHT, *What Was It? Fishing Vessel, The Magic Box*, Kestrel Books, 1987, Copyright © Kit Wright 1984, 1987. Reproduced by permission of Penguin Books Ltd; CHARLOTTE ZOLOTOW, *Pink Azalea*, from *River Winding* by Charlotte Zolotow (Thomas Y.Crowell) Copyright © 1970 by Charlotte Zolotow, by permission of Harper & Row, Publishers Inc and William Heinemann Ltd.

Every effort has been made to trace the ownership of copyright material in this book, but in the event of any question arising as to the use of any material, the publishers will be pleased to make the necessary correction in future editions of the book.